THE
ARCHITECTURE
SCHOOL
SURVIVAL GUIDE

LAURENCE KING

Published in 2015 by
Laurence King Publishing Ltd
361–373 City Road
London EC1V 1LR
United Kingdom
email: enquiries@laurenceking.com
www.laurenceking.com

A catalogue record for this book is available from the British Library.

ISBN: 978 178067 579 4

Design concept: Twosheds Design
Book design: The Urban Ant Ltd

Printed in China

THE ARCHITECTURE SCHOOL SURVIVAL GUIDE

IAIN JACKSON

LAURENCE KING PUBLISHING

INTRODUCTION

This architecture survival guide will help you and your drawings to communicate more effectively. Each page offers essential advice on the fundamentals of architecture – use these tips, principles and guides to inform your own designs. So often, during a critique (or jury), the student spends too much time explaining the basics of his or her ideas and countering misinterpretations, leaving very little opportunity to discuss the architectural merits and content of the proposal. Don't let basic graphical omissions and simple oversights detract from otherwise good schemes.

The main aims of this book are to assist you in your studio designs and to improve your ability to communicate and express an idea. Most of what you will read and observe here is discussed every day in architecture schools around the world – use it as an aide-memoire before tutorials and critiques so that you can participate in the more enjoyable and challenging task of designing spaces and effortlessly imparting what you want to convey.

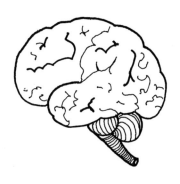

all that
scratchini

is makin me itch

I LOVE YOU

GOT TO GO

THE WORLD AROUND US

BECOME AN EXPLORER/
URBAN DAWDLER/FLÂNEUR

1 Photocopy or download and print a map of your neighbourhood, district or city.

2 Take a marker pen and sign your name across the map.

3 Your signature is the route you must take through the area shown on the map.

4 Walk the route and record your observations, trying to remain faithful to the route created by the signature.

The aim of this exercise is to re-explore a familiar place, taking a route that you would not normally take, and without any purpose other than to observe, explore and encounter the new and unexpected. Document your exploration by taking photographs or sketching. Be prepared to get lost and to negotiate your way through buildings and spaces. You will learn to see your city afresh, come across interesting side streets and back alleys, make unexpected connections and cross thresholds that lead into new realms ...

KEEP A NOTEBOOK/DIARY OF EVENTS

Keeping a sketchbook is essential, but in addition always keep a notebook/diary. Don't buy a purpose-made diary with a week-per-page arrangement and list of national holidays and hat sizes at the front; instead you need a lined/squared notebook – Moleskine, Magma or a similar brand – about 140 × 90 millimetres (5½ × 3½ inches) in size. Use this book to record your thoughts, ideas and dreams. You should also use it to plan your working day, and to write down your model-making shopping lists, library references and tutorial notes. Most such notebooks also have a pocket at the back in which you can store tickets, contact cards and mementos. Number and date each and every page. Aim to fill one notebook per month. These little books will become repositories of your discoveries. They will also document your design process, which is crucial at architecture school.

SET SOME GOALS AND MAKE A LIST: WHAT DO I WANT TO ACHIEVE TODAY/BY FRIDAY/THE END OF THE MONTH/BEFORE I DIE?

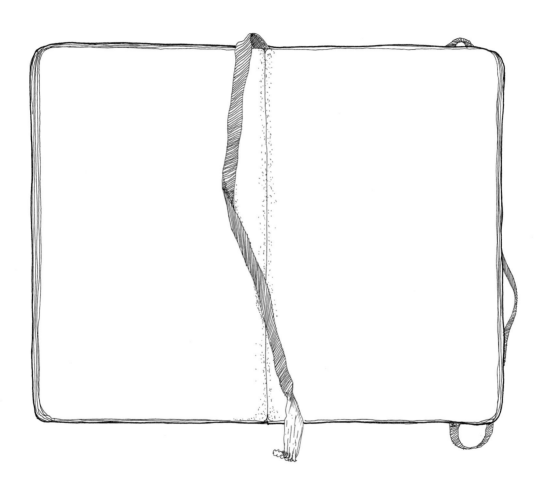

FIELD TRIPS:
BECOME AN URBANAUT

Organized field trips are an essential part of an architect's education. Not only can you explore a new city and all of its charms, but also deepen friendships and form new ones. A field trip gives you the chance to break away from the familiarity of the studio and to be exposed to new, stimulating ideas, systems and buildings. Take the opportunity to sketch and photograph incessantly.

Try to also build in a weekly local trip in which you visit exhibitions, galleries, concerts and places in your local city. This will give your mind a break from your studio projects and expose you to a wider circle of contacts and modes of thinking.

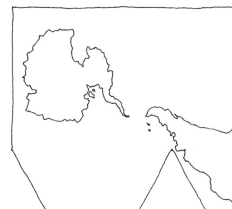

EVERY ARCHITECT SHOULD EXPERIENCE THE FOLLOWING CITIES:

❶ Athens
❷ Ahmedabad
❸ Barcelona
❹ Berlin
❺ Brasilia
❻ Chandigarh
❼ Chicago
❽ Copenhagen
❾ Florence
❿ Helsinki
⓫ Hong Kong
⓬ Las Vegas
⓭ Lagos
⓮ New York
⓯ Paris
⓰ Rome
⓱ Shanghai
⓲ Stockholm
⓳ Tokyo
⓴ Vienna

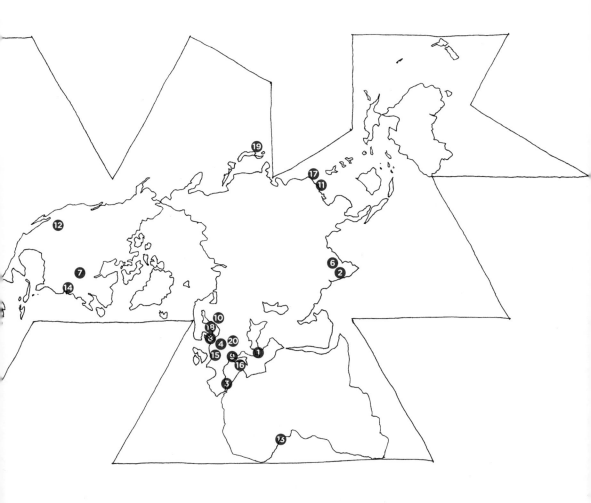

A PHOTOGRAPH OF A BUILDING IS NOT THE BUILDING

Be very wary of architectural photographs published in glossy journals and hardback books. A photograph of a building is not *the* building – rather, it is a highly choreographed and staged image. The building will have been photographed from a specific angle, in perfect lighting conditions and looking pristine set against a perfect blue sky. The image might also have been altered to force perspectives, or to remove blemishes and other perceived 'flaws'. By all means enjoy the impact and glamour of the architectural photograph, but always try to visit a building, or at least consult the plans and sections to gain further understanding of it.

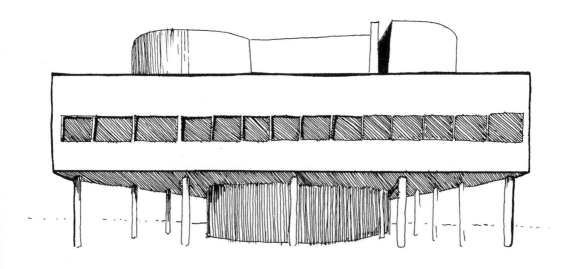

SKETCH

Although we live in an age in which high-quality rendering and 3D computer modelling are readily accessible, there is no match for a quick sketch. The sketch seduces potential clients over dinner, quickly explains ideas to colleagues and other design professionals, and helps to resolve conflicts and misunderstandings on the building site. Sketching is also highly enjoyable – but it is a skill that needs to be developed and maintained. 10–15 minutes practice per day will reap some outstanding results.

Start with a very soft pencil (9B) or charcoal. Spend at least 2–3 minutes just looking at the subject matter before you put pencil to paper. Relax and don't worry about the results. Sketching is really about observation and 'learning to see'; it is not about showpieces.

READ

It is essential that you read books on and about architecture and architects. There is a great tradition of architectural publishing – explore your libraries, seek out second-hand bookshops and become a bibliophile. Set aside a minimum reading time of 30 minutes per day. A good knowledge of architectural journals, monographs and theoretical texts will help you to add meaning, historical context and greater sophistication to your own designs.

THE VERNACULAR

We can learn a lot from looking at the vernacular architecture of a place – especially in terms of materials and forms that respond to climate and character. There is a beauty and a timeless quality to this architecture. The corners, lintels (horizontal supports across the tops of doors and windows), sills and openings are important on every building. Here, specially cut stones form the corners – not only giving strength to the construction, but also serving as 'capital letters' and 'full stops', helping to frame the architecture and punctuate the form. Always give special attention to the places where materials and forms join or change shape. In practical terms these places need attention to keep the weather out, but they are also important visually and need to be considered when designing the façade. The use of local materials and forms will also enrich your designs.

DENSITY

Density can express lots of different conditions – and it is a frequently misunderstood concept. For example, a high-rise building does not necessarily indicate high density if it is positioned in a large tract of open land. Look at the three examples opposite – they all have the same number of dwelling units per hectare, but each presents very different living conditions for the occupants. A mid-rise solution can provide a shared and private garden space along with a variety of housing types and sizes. The number of residents per hectare is a more useful statistic than the number of dwellings per hectare and, in either case, it is essential to review how the housing and the people are distributed across the area available.

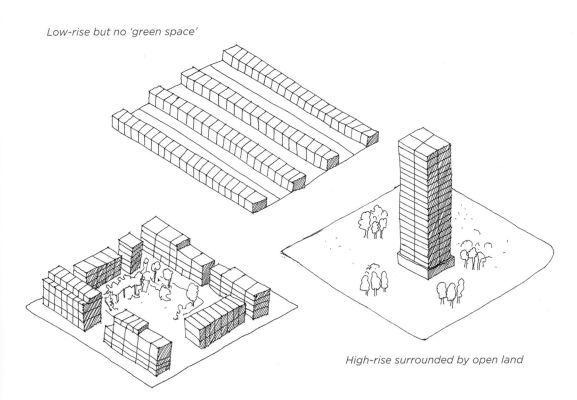

Low-rise but no 'green space'

High-rise surrounded by open land

Mid-rise and mixed use with overlooked communal space

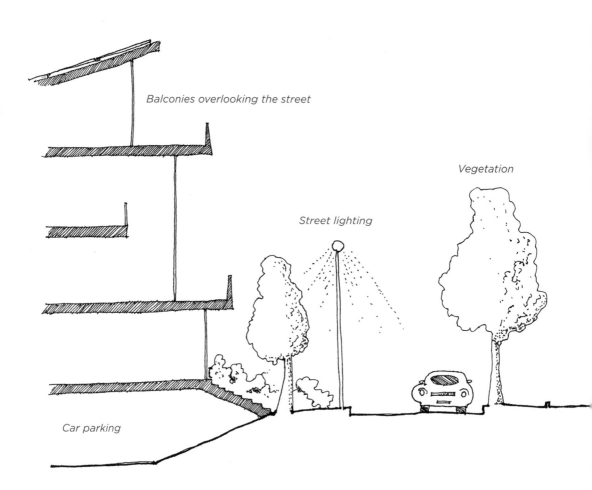

Balconies overlooking the street

Vegetation

Street lighting

Car parking

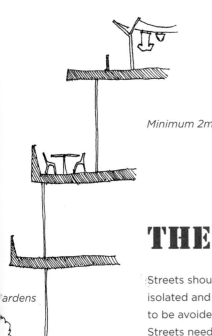

Minimum 2m (6ft) balcony space

ardens

THE STREET

Streets should be exciting places that are full of life and activity. Dark, isolated and infrequently used streets that are geared towards the car are to be avoided and are more likely to be dangerous and unpleasant places. Streets need space for pedestrians, cyclists and vehicular traffic. They should be well-lit, tree-lined and equipped with robust furniture – but not too many railings or traffic-calming devices. Mixed use – an 'active street front' including spaces for working, retail and leisure at ground level and housing above – should be encouraged. Car parking needs to be properly addressed, footpaths provided and public space properly designed.

CONTOURS AND SLOPE

Always try to exploit a site's natural attributes, especially any changes in level. While developers and house-builders may regard sloping sites as too problematic, they have enormous potential for exciting architecture. If you run the design parallel to the site contours then the solution will be easier to build and less expensive – it may also benefit from a panoramic view (as in **Ⓐ**). By placing the floor plate perpendicular to the contour of a slope you can develop half-levels and double-height interior spaces (**Ⓑ**), perhaps raise the building on piloti (**Ⓒ**) or even cantilever out from the slope. Other options include partially burying the proposal and giving access to the roof (**Ⓓ**). The earth removed to make way for the building can be used to fill the terrain elsewhere.

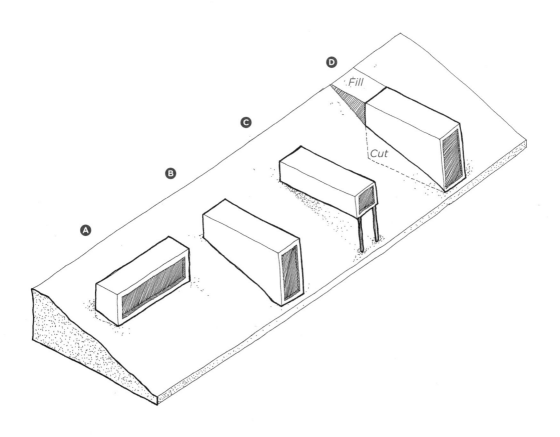

PRECEDENT STUDIES

Every building is a bespoke prototype and no two buildings will have the same details – it is nevertheless essential that you learn how other architects have approached and solved similar problems.

Three elements should be considered in every precedent study:

❶ *Functional typology:* if you are designing a museum, look at how other museums are designed and planned. How are the exhibition spaces arranged? Is there a prescribed route or are visitors expected to explore?

❷ *Material typology:* look at the details and tectonic solutions of buildings that have been constructed from the materials you wish to use.

❸ *Formal typology:* if your site is very narrow look at other projects with a narrow footprint; if you are planning to use a courtyard type, then study other courtyard buildings, irrespective of their functions.

Present your findings and attempt to summarize the important aspects that you will use in your scheme. You are not 'copying' another building, but rather applying the same principles.

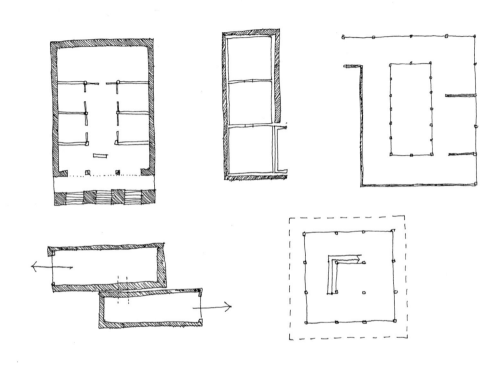

Functional typology: Gather examples of the same functional type and compare how they are arranged. Here are five museum types – each fulfilling the same function but designed in completely different ways. They are drawn at the same scale to enable comparison.

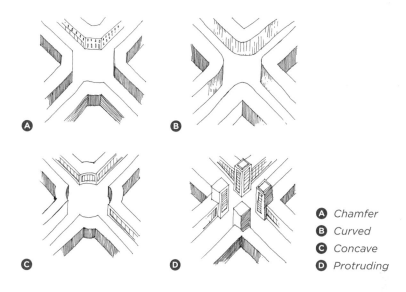

A Chamfer
B Curved
C Concave
D Protruding

TURNING A CORNER

Corners are important in the formation of streets and blocks. They need to be designed carefully. A corner is the junction of two streets and as a result there are implications for traffic routes, but also great opportunities for the architecture to respond. How will your design address the corner? Will it be celebratory – a kind of capital letter for the street – or will it soften the harsh edge with a 45-degree chamfer (sloping edge) or curve?

100 CORNERS

Fill a sketchbook with 100 drawings
of buildings that create a street corner.
How do the materials and form respond
to the corner, if at all?

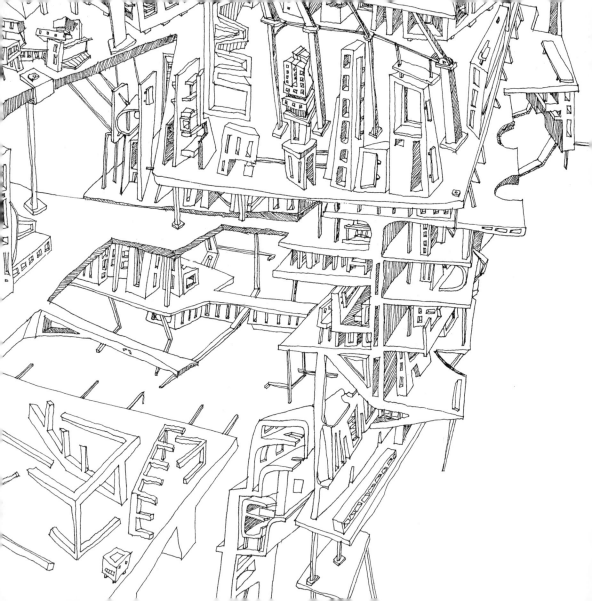

DRAWING FOR FUN

It is good to draw without really having an agenda, a design problem to solve or a subject to represent. Just drawing, doodling or creating imaginary places, buildings and creatures are good ways of relaxing and allowing the subconscious to emerge. When you are stuck with a problem or are feeling a little demotivated, start drawing your imaginary streets and buildings. More often than not, you will gain greater clarity and generate an exciting set of drawings.

THE SITE PLAN

Always include in your presentation a site plan showing the wider neighbourhood. Show the key landmarks, as well as any natural features such as rivers, so that locating your site will be easier for people viewing your proposals. You could also include directional arrows and annotation to indicate how your proposal relates to existing views and transport routes, and how it connects streets and districts. North must always point upwards and site drawings are usually shown at 1:1,250 or 1:2,500 scale (see p. 49).

1 Major natural features (e.g. rivers)

2 Transportation (e.g. trains, trams, ferries, canals)

3 Green spaces/parks

4 Public spaces/monuments

5 Important historical buildings

6 Districts (e.g. northern quarter/red light district/ghetto/central business district)

7 Views/vantage points

8 Problems (noise/busy roads/missed opportunities)

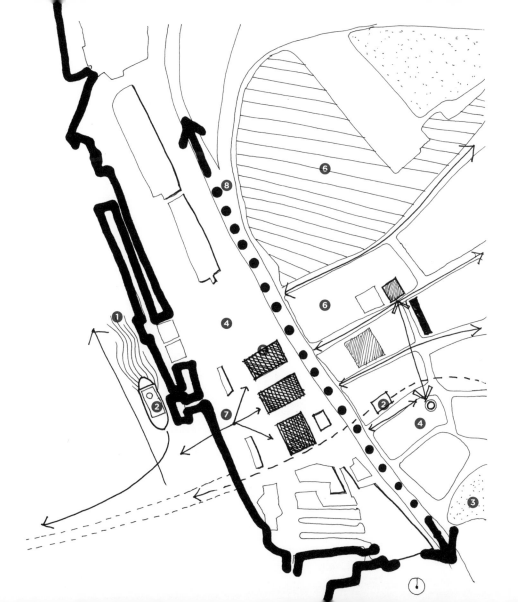

THE MUNDANE

Keep a look out for 'sublime ugliness', the banal and the everyday. When you find it, make a sketch of it and celebrate it. This is not praise of mediocrity, but about observing how we live and about improving the overall quality of design. Not everything should be iconic or attention-grabbing – try to look at the quotidian through fresh eyes and seek to deliver quality design in the everyday things we use and spaces we inhabit.

THE SUM OF THE PARTS

In architecture we need to take the ordinary and the quotidian and arrange them in ways that transform them. We need the minimum intervention for the maximum effect. Merely solving the utilitarian requirements of architecture is not enough. 1 plus 1 should always equal 3. You must get more out than you put in.

THINKING ABOUT SCALE

STREET WIDTH-TO-BUILDING HEIGHT RATIO

The relationship between the width of a street and the height of the surrounding buildings has a major effect on how a street feels to its users. A medieval town centre with narrow alleys and overhanging balconies is intimate and exciting to explore. In a modern metropolis, however, the building heights may be as much as ten times larger than the streets are wide, dramatically reducing sunlight at street level, and causing massive overshadows and wind tunnels. Pedestrians also find it difficult to cross these streets, due to traffic and gusts of wind. On the other hand, overly wide streets with single- or two-storey dwellings lack the energy of a busy thoroughfare and are often wasteful, as more roads, services and landscaping are required per building. Land value often dictates building height and density, but you should be aware of how your design will impact upon the streetscape and attempt to create an appropriate density, with streets that are usable and enjoyable places in which to spend time.

45

SURFACE AREA-TO-VOLUME RATIO

A building with a large surface area-to-volume ratio can result in more views, openings and natural light penetrating deep into the building. On the negative side it means there is more surface area through which heat can be lost (in cold climates) or gained (in hot ones). In a hot climate, however, there is more opportunity to benefit from ventilation and wind cooling – provided of course that the walls and openings are shaded from the sun. If a small surface area-to-volume ratio is desired then using a sphere would create the optimum ratio (but this is a form with limited functional qualities). Type **G** has a very large surface area-to-volume ratio and, if used in a hot climate, could allow more shading, cooling courtyards and cross-ventilation. Type **H** is frequently used for hotels as it offers a large surface area (permitting windows in each room) in a relatively compact plan, as well as a central band suitable for housing communal facilities and receptions.

AREA	SURFACE AREA	AREA	SURFACE AREA
A 16	16	**E** 16	32
B 16	20	**F** 16	64
C 16	34	**G** 16	34
D 16	30	**H** 16	34

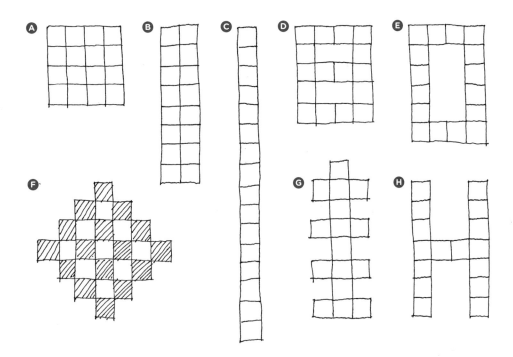

DRAWING TO SCALE

We draw buildings using a system that renders them smaller than life-size. We call this 'drawing to scale'. For example, a scale of 1:50 means that the drawing of the building is 50 times smaller than the real thing. Or you can think of it as 1 centimetre (⅓ inch) on the drawing equalling 50 centimetres (19½ inches) in reality. We draw at different scales to show different amounts of detail and to convey different sets of information.

Generally we start with the site plans and overall building plans. These drawings show the building's location and the basic plan layouts. As the design progresses the scale increases and we start to look at the building detail and construction. It is important to include the relevant amount of detail for the scale selected. Architectural drawings are produced at the scales listed opposite. (Scales such as 1:25 and 1:33 are sometimes shown on scale rules, but these are for engineering projects and are never used for architectural drawings.) Some countries use an imperial scale of feet and inches – the same principles apply.

SCALE	DRAWING TYPE	WHAT YOU SHOULD INCLUDE
1:1,250 or 1:2,500	Site plans and site analysis	Street layouts, basic outline of the site.
1:200/1:100	General arrangement drawings	Block outlines of the building proposal. Landscaping and context must be shown. Materials may be labelled and furniture can be included. For small buildings this information should be shown at 1:100 scale.
1:50	Detailed drawings	The building design will be resolved and basic construction elements should be shown, including the position of insulation and structural members. All rooms should be fully labelled and should show furniture layouts and materials.
1:20	Construction	Useful for showing how an entire wall section will be constructed.
1:10/1:5	Details	Fully detailed construction drawings often incorporating specialist or subcontractor drawings. All building components should be labelled and cross-referenced to the 1:200 or 1:100 general arrangement drawings.
1:1	Prototypes/CNC (computer numerically controlled) routing/ computer-aided manufacture/templates	CAD (computer-aided design) drawings may be used to produce the building components. Ornamentation and stonemasons' templates for more traditional buildings will be produced at this scale.

IT'S ALL ABOUT SCALE

The size and proportion of each component of a design often determine the success of a piece of architecture. The difference between good and bad architecture is a matter of centimetres or inches. In general, we scale our surroundings by the human form, especially entrances, doorways and floor-to-ceiling heights. Certain places are designed on a monumental scale to invoke awe and wonder (such as cathedrals); other spaces are small to create intimacy and feelings of security (such as a 'snug').

Some architects have attempted to use specific proportions and dimensions. The best-known proportioning system is Le Corbusier's Modulor, which relates the dimensions of a human figure to the Fibonacci sequence (a mathematical sequence in which each number is the sum of the two preceding ones). However, scale is relative and difficult to meaningfully quantify in this way. You should, instead, consult Lewis Carroll's Victorian fantasy novel *Alice's Adventures in Wonderland*, which provides a better insight into the importance of relative scale.

SCALING THE CUBE

When the external dimensions of a building are changed the volume does not change by the same proportions. For example, a building that is 2 × 2 × 2 metres (6 × 6 × 6 feet) will have a volume of 8 m³ (216 cu ft) whereas a 4 × 4 × 4 metres (13 × 13 × 13 feet) building will have a volume of 64 m³ (2196 cu ft). In other words, in a larger cube you get a lot more volume per surface area. The larger volume could therefore be considered more economical and efficient. On the downside it will require more heating and cooling.

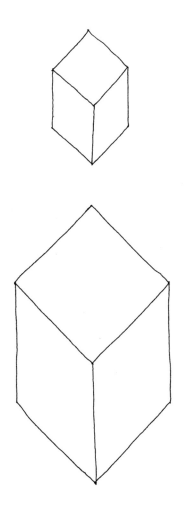

BUILDING COMPONENTS AND DESIGN CONSIDERATIONS

THE COLUMN, THE BEAM AND THE WALL

It would not be overly reductive and simplistic to say that most architecture can be created using the column, the beam and the wall. By carefully considering the spacing, thickness, rhythm, composition and materiality of these three elements, it is possible to compose some fine architectural solutions. If we add the ramp and the staircase, as well as doors and windows in the walls, we have a kit of parts that will answer most architectural questions. Do not be afraid of using simple, right-angled, rectilinear solutions. Use the arc, circle and ellipse with extreme caution.

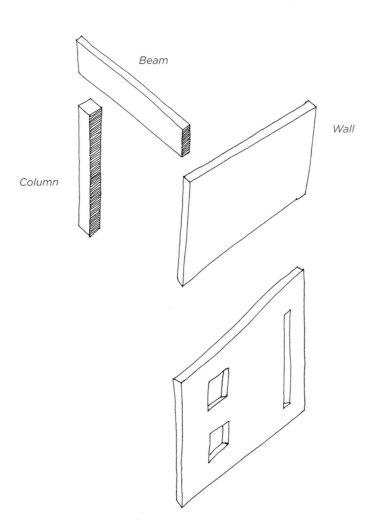

Beam

Column

Wall

POSITIONING THE COLUMN

Do not simply lay out a structural grid of columns – think about where they should be placed in relation to the walls, partitions and openings. A pilaster (column projecting from a wall) can help to demarcate space and boundaries. If the column is always embedded within the wall, and therefore hidden, we miss the chance to express the structure and the rhythmical qualities it can bring to a building. Is the wall even necessary?

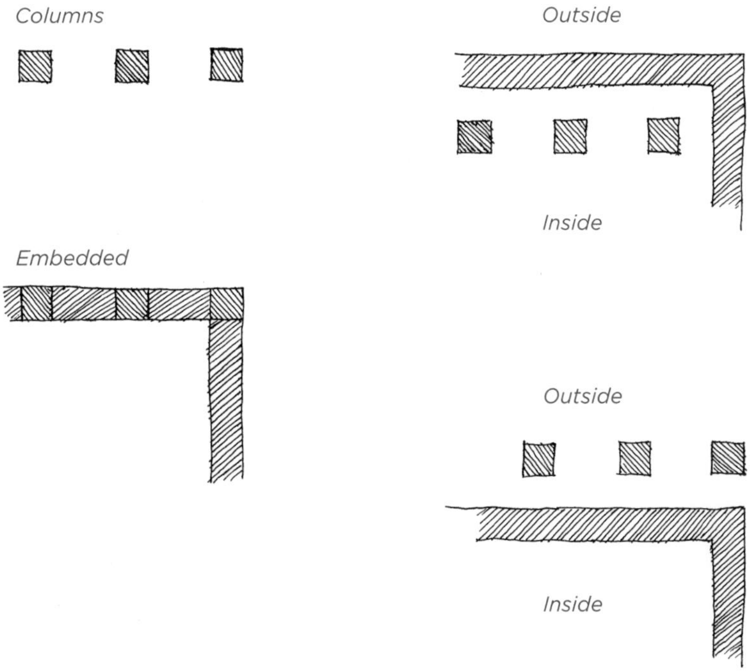

Columns

Embedded

Outside

Inside

Outside

Inside

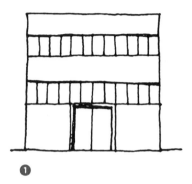

❶

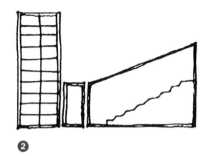

❷

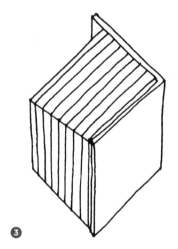

❸

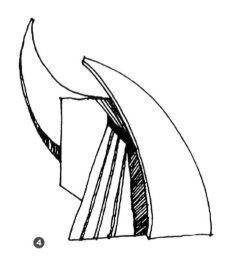

❹

QUESTIONS OF FORM

How will you generate an architectural form?
Where do your ideas come from?
Will your form be derived from a response to function?
Is architecture about sculpture and expressive shapes?

These are the questions that you will grapple with throughout your life
as an architect.

You can perhaps think about four ways of generating form:

1 Fit all of the building's requirements into a neat, 'functional' box.

2 Express the building's functions, so that each programme has its own distinct form, e.g. a lecture theatre in one form and a library in another.

3 Attempt to figuratively express the building's function through its form, e.g. design a library building to look a little like a book.

4 Ignore the function and use some other means to generate form independently of function. The form could be developed as a sculptural response and the function forced to fit it.

THE ENVELOPE

The building envelope distinguishes the inside from the outside; it is the actual form of the building and it defines the volume and spaces within. The envelope must meet several demands:

1 It has to be permeable in certain parts and impermeable in others. It has to let people in, whilst keeping rain and wind out.

2 It must resist damp emerging from the earth.

3 It must attempt to modify the air temperature, ideally to within the very narrow band that humans find comfortable.

4 It must let in light at certain places and also enable some air to enter the building to ventilate it (this may be highly controlled using mechanical systems or done simply by opening a window).

5 It must also allow the entry of services (water, gas, electricity, telecommunications) and the disposal of waste (sewage, rainwater, smoke).

6 It should be durable and strong enough to withstand winds and storms, as well as to keep out unwanted visitors such as ants, rats and human intruders.

7 It should weather gracefully, ideally getting better-looking as it ages, and be easy to maintain and clean.

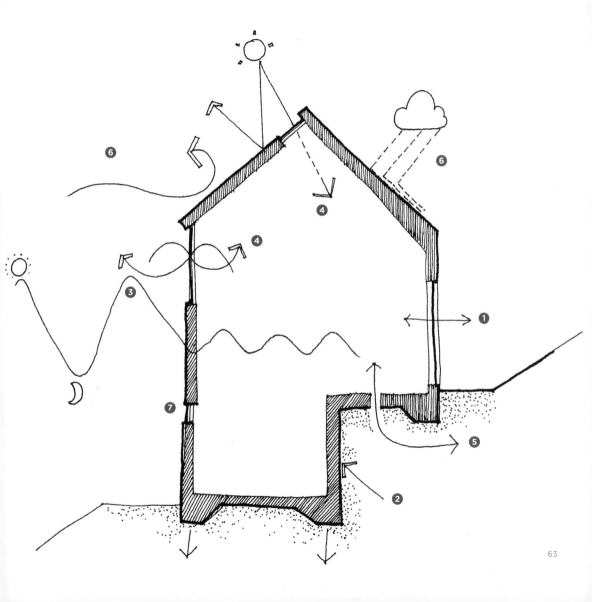

THE WALL

Generally, there are two types of wall:

❶ *The load-bearing wall:* this type carries its own weight and also supports the floors, roof and contents of the building. It keeps out the weather and incorporates an insulating material. It is a simple and successful model that is commonly used on small buildings and houses. It must be made of a material capable of carrying this load. The wall thickness is generally proportional to the building's height: a taller building will require thicker walls, reducing the usable floorspace and increasing the amount of material required. Openings are formed by punching holes in the wall; lintels or arches hold up the wall above them.

❷ *The non-load-bearing wall:* this method uses a series of columns and beams to create a frame which supports the floors, roof and building contents. The exterior wall either carries its own weight and is 'tied back' to the frame or is entirely supported by the frame structure – it carries no other loads, hence its name. This method achieves greater height without the loss of floor area and permits the use of non-structural materials such as glazing on the façade. Openings can be large and are not dependent on lintels or arches.

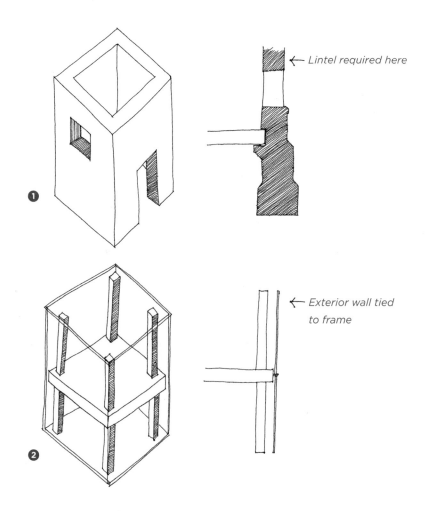

1. _Lintel required here_

2. _Exterior wall tied to frame_

THE WINDOW

A window is an opening in the wall that is usually transparent or semi-opaque and is frequently constructed with glass panels held in a frame. Windows have several functions: to provide a room with natural ventilation; to let light into a room; to create a view out from a building; and/or to create a view into a building (such as a shop window).

Window settings: think about where your window will sit within the thickness of the wall. This decision will often inform the character of the façade. Setting the window back into the wall creates a sense of stability, whereas a window flush to the outside face gives a more streamlined finish (but is also more likely to stain below the windowsill). A deep interior windowsill can also be used as a seat, and splayed walls can help to bring more light into the room as well as drawing attention to the view.

Frames: the window frame also needs consideration. A slender metal frame will convey a different meaning from one created by leaded glass with timber casements on vertical hinges. Dotted lines are used in drawings to show opening lights and hinge positions.

Shapes: long horizontal windows frame a panoramic view, whereas tall slender windows throw light further back into the room and create a sense of height in the interior. Wrapping a window around the corner of a building is dramatic – but difficult to achieve with load-bearing walls.

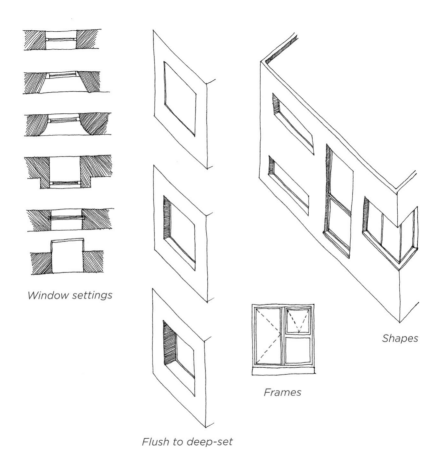

Window settings

Flush to deep-set

Frames

Shapes

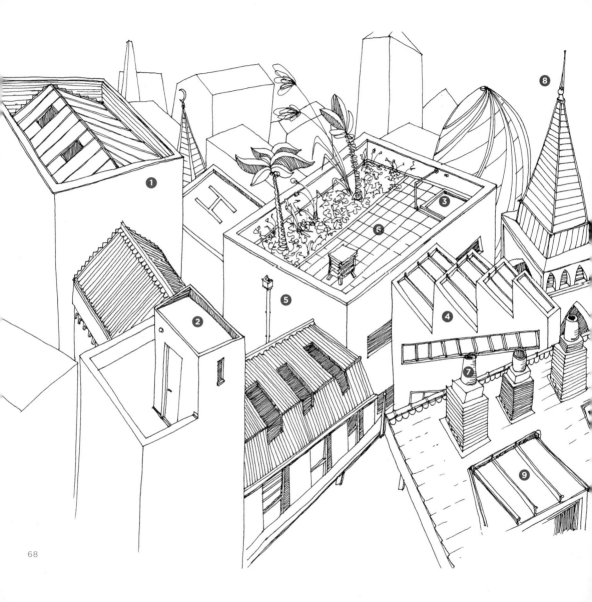

THE ROOF

Sometimes referred to as the fifth elevation, the roof is an often neglected component of building design. Try to put this area back into use by creating a garden, a space for energy generation or a habitat for wildlife.

1 Hide a pitched roof with a parapet wall (don't forget the flashing between the wall and the roof).

2 Access to the roof is required. Trapdoors are to be avoided.

3 Add barriers and handrails where trapdoors must be used.

4 Factories and studios need even, north-facing light without shadows. The sawtooth roof is ideal for this purpose.

5 Rainwater needs to be removed from roofs. The pipes could be set into the wall or be expressed on the façade.

6 Use the roofspace as a living space.

7 Fumes can be expelled through the roof.

8 The roof as beacon and eye-catcher. It can be used to draw attention to the building and to aid navigation through a town.

9 The roof can be used for storage.

THE STAIRCASE

The staircase enables us to move from one floor to another. It also offers exciting design possibilities, both as an object in its own right and as a result of the views and vantage points it can offer.

Avoid the spiral staircase – it uses just as much room as a straight staircase and, in many instances the space around it cannot be put to use.

1 Round the bottom step: it makes it easier for the person stepping off the stair to turn the corner.

2 It is a good idea (where space allows) to create a small stairwell between flights of stairs. This allows more light to travel down the staircase and makes for a more exciting journey.

3 Put a window at the landing. This not only brings light into the staircase, but also gives a view out from a resting point.

4 The space in front of a staircase should be at least as long as the staircase is wide.

5 Put a skylight above the staircase to wash the space with light.

6 Always cut a section through the staircase to ensure that you have enough headroom.

7 Stairs should have a riser of 200mm (8in) and a tread of 250mm (10in).

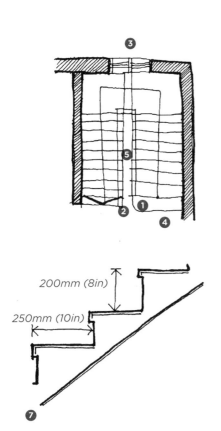

200mm (8in)

250mm (10in)

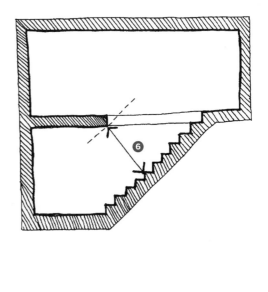

CIRCULATION AND SANITATION

When planning a larger building try to group together the vertical circulation (stairs and elevators, lobbies and toilets). It is convenient for the visitors to the building and permits efficient construction, as vertical service ducts and pipe-runs can be easily installed along with the lift shafts and stairs. In all your designs try to stack service rooms such as kitchens and toilets one above the other, floor by floor, to benefit from efficient pipe-runs.

❶ Lift
❷ Services shaft
❸ Cleaner's cupboard

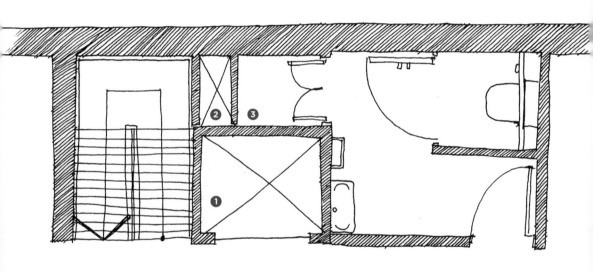

BUILDING ORIENTATION

In temperate and cold climates orientate your building to exploit sunlight and the heat it generates. Besides creating a more sustainable building, careful orientation can also improve the quality of the spaces and the general well-being of their occupants. Bedrooms should face east so that they get the early morning sun. Gardens should, ideally, face south and rooms facing that direction should be shaded and ventilated to avoid overheating. Living rooms/kitchen-sink windows should face west. Rooms that don't require any light, such as garages and bathrooms, should face north, as should workshops and studios, which benefit from shadowless light. Regardless of the building's function, think about the effect of sunlight and shadows on your proposal.

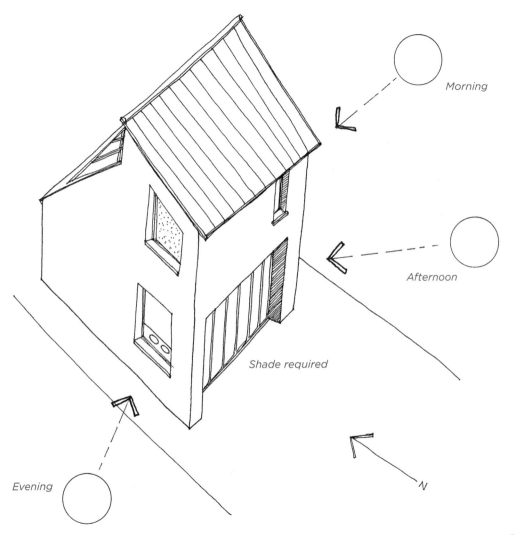

Morning

Afternoon

Shade required

Evening

N

INSULATION

In temperate and cold climates insulation is an essential part of construction, to reduce energy demands and to increase comfort. But where should you put it and with what consequence? The example opposite looks at a basic wall section. Example A shows the insulation on the inside face of a wall. The main problem with this approach is interstitial condensation (condensation forming within a wall). An effective vapour barrier is required to prevent moisture travelling from the inside from condensing when it touches the cold outer wall at point ❶. The advantage of this approach, however, is that the room will warm up quickly and energy will not be spent heating the building fabric, as in example B, which shows the insulation on the outside of the main structure. This will need protecting with an outer layer of material, such as render or timber. Interstitial condensation is far less likely with this approach, but a vapour barrier is still strongly recommended at points ❷ or ❸. The room will take longer to warm up, but the structure will also act as a heatstore, resulting in less extreme temperature changes throughout the day.

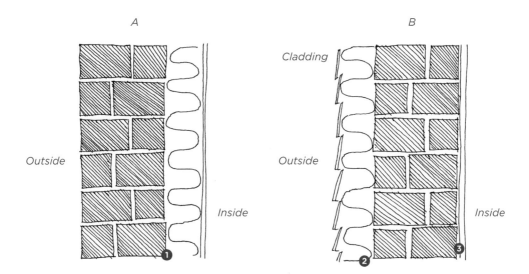

A

Outside

Inside

➊

B

Cladding

Outside

Inside

➋ ➌

THE DOOR

A door is a piece of moveable wall. It enables access into a space and can, equally, deny it to preserve security, privacy and warmth.

1 The conventional door is hinged on one side and opens into the room – so space has to be left to accommodate its swing. Note how the door sits within its own frame (architrave), which adds protection and provides a better finish against the plasterwork.

2 An alternative approach is to create a pocket in the wall in which to slide the door. The wall thickness will need to be increased to accommodate it.

3 A drawbridge is always exciting, as are roller-shutters and bi-folding doors.

4 The off-centred pivot door also has architectural potential, particularly very large doors of this type, which can give the appearance of the entire façade being opened up.

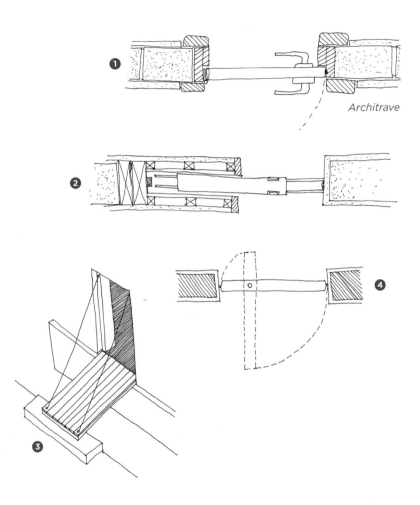

Architrave

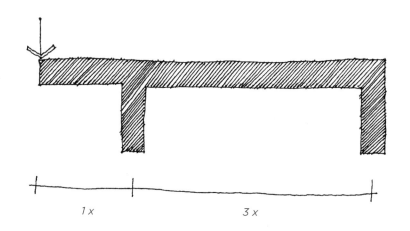

1 x   3 x

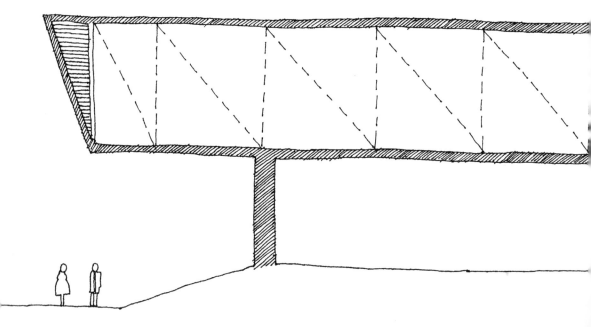

THE CANTILEVER

A cantilever is a structural member that is anchored at one end only. It enables the construction of overhanging structures, which can be spatially and visually very exciting. Generally speaking a cantilever needs a back span that is three times longer than the 'floating' element (although there are many exceptions to this rule).

Think of the cantilevered element as a truss. Sloping the ground plane away from the building and leaning the face of the cantilever outwards may also accentuate the architectural gymnastics.

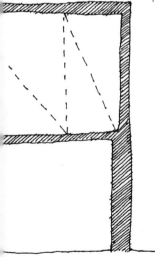

SOMETIMES WHEN WE TOUCH/ DON'T TOUCH ME

The buildings designed by Indian architect Charles Correa (b. 1930) are experienced through the 'soles of the feet' – architecture is not just visual, it is multisensory, and the parts we touch are particularly important. The eye confirms what the hand already knows. Seating should not conduct heat; door handles should fit well into the hand; handrails and balustrades should be carefully detailed and be comfortable to grip. Some places, however, should have minimum human contact – where possible remove from public toilets all soap dispensers and doors that are manually operated. How do your designs sound as well as look, and what tactile properties do they possess?

MATERIALS

It is possible to think about architecture independently of its material properties. We can resolve a plan and generate ideas – but it is wise to consider the materials as early as possible in the design/concept stage. You should not simply apply materials to a form like wallpaper; instead you should work with their inherent qualities and the form should emerge, in part, from the materials chosen. As well as looking good, materials should be durable, affordable and easy to fabricate on site. Joints, seams and unit sizes should be coordinated so that the façade forms an ensemble of materials and awkward junctions are avoided. New materials can lead to new forms and methods of construction – but proceed cautiously until they have been tried and tested.

Do not make the mistake of using lots of materials in one building – limit your palette to no more than three for the building envelope.

SUSTAINABILITY

The most sustainable approach to construction, is in fact, not to build anything at all. But if you must design a building then it should be compact, passive rather than technologically driven (a significant amount of energy is required to produce a photovoltaic cell), carefully orientated to maximize natural light, and built from materials that are and can be recycled and have been produced locally. Ensure that insulation is continuous around the building envelope and that 'cold bridges' are avoided in cold climates (a 'cold bridge' is an un-insulated part of the building fabric that conducts heat from the inside to the outside; it is also likely to encourage damp as warm, moist air condenses onto its surface). In hot climates air conditioning is now the norm, along with glazed façades – but this is not the way to go as we approach the post-oil age. Space and water heating are two areas that are easy to address whilst using conventional construction.

1 Harvest rainwater and use it for washing clothes, bathing and flushing toilets.

2 Harvest bathwater and use it for watering gardens.

3 Heat water using a wood-fired boiler, solar panels and an electric immersion heater.

4 A ground–air heat exchanger can provide both warm and cooled air.

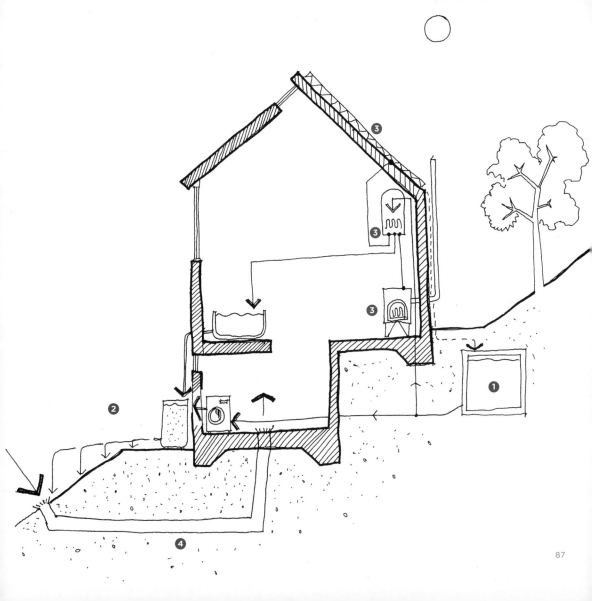

DIGITAL HERITAGE

Present your work to the world. Document your findings and publish them. Set up a blog and record your explorations. Photograph your city, neighbourhood and streets and develop an archive. You can refer back to this information and begin to observe how your surroundings are slowly changing as new buildings emerge and old ones are demolished.

BACK UP ALL
YOUR PHOTOGRAPHS AND
DIGITIZED DRAWINGS DAILY.
DO IT NOW.

COMMUNICATIONS

WHO ARE YOU DRAWING FOR?

We produce drawings for a number of reasons. Some drawings are used to help the client understand what kind of building they are getting; others are used to set the sale price of a building or as a set of guidelines for construction. As architects, we produce yet others during the design process to help us think about the spaces and forms we are creating. The way we draw affects the way we design. Develop drawings and diagrams that communicate your concept or big idea. Don't be afraid of expressive and experimental modes of mark-making in the first instance. It is equally important that you do not jump to the computer too soon. Instead, explore an idea using sketches: switch between plan, section, detail and rough 3D drawings to enable a set of ideas to emerge.

Some drawings for presentation purposes are used to 'sell' the scheme. If a building does not look good on paper, it will certainly not look good when it is built. Always think about who your drawings are for and tailor them accordingly.

LINEWEIGHTS

The thickness of a line on a drawing is very important because it makes the drawing more legible, creates the illusion of depth and conveys a visual hierarchy of importance. The ground line must be very heavy – without it the building looks like it is 'floating' on the page. Thicker lines are used on elevations to show objects that are 'closer' to the viewer, and sometimes to indicate shadows, and on plans they are used for structural components and the building envelope. On sections, the thickest line is reserved for the components that are 'sliced through', whereas objects viewed in elevation, beyond the section line, are drawn in the thinnest lines. If lineweights are not used properly then a drawing has a tendency to look flat and illegible.

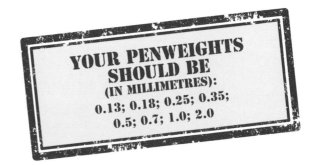

YOUR PENWEIGHTS
SHOULD BE
(IN MILLIMETRES):
0.13; 0.18; 0.25; 0.35;
0.5; 0.7; 1.0; 2.0

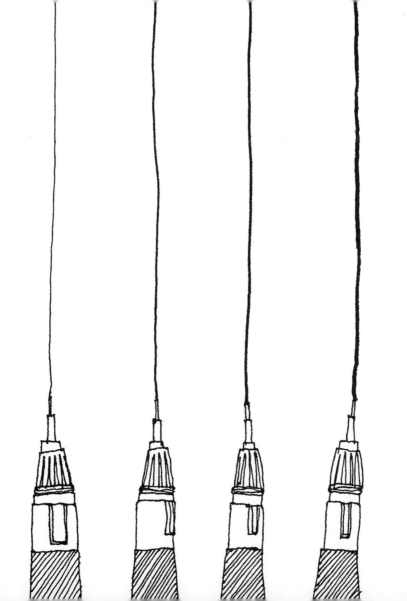

ANNOTATE YOUR DRAWINGS

Give your drawing a title, and state what it is, such as 'A–A Section'. Label the rooms, indicate materials, and add notes or arrows to show views, routes and design intentions.

Without this information drawings are subject to varied interpretations. The image opposite, for example, could be of a light bulb, or of someone bending over in the bath. Notes remove uncertainty and eliminate ambiguity.

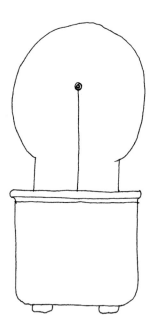

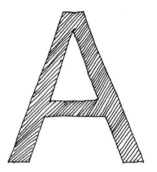

Serif *Sans serif*

FONTS

The font you choose is important: for example, Garamond (serif) and Helvetica (sans serif) communicate completely different things. The choice of font is part of the message you are attempting to convey. A serif font is indebted to the stonemason's chisel, the serifs being a legacy of how the stone was carved. The sans serif font discards these anachronistic references. Serif implies the 'establishment', tradition and longevity, whereas sans serif denotes clarity and modernity. It is not a case of what we say, but rather how we say it.

THE AXONOMETRIC

Use your building plans to construct an axonometric projection (also known as an axo: a 3D drawing without perspective). It is a great way to express your ideas because it is to scale, demonstrates the spatial qualities of your proposal, and can be used to show the plan, elevation, section and even construction details in one place. The axo is a useful drawing to show to people not familiar with plans and sections. Draw all of your projects in axo and demonstrate that you know how the building will operate and what it will look like.

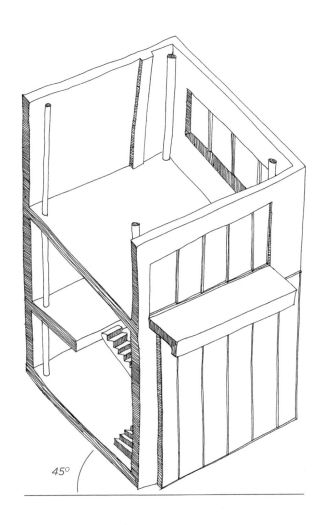

45°

THE PLAN

The plan is a highly abstract mode of representation. Imagine cutting horizontally through a building about 1 metre (3 feet) above floor level – that is what we are attempting to draw in a plan. The plan does not deal with the spatial qualities of the architecture, but it is useful for laying out furniture and working out how the space can be divided up, for example for rental purposes.

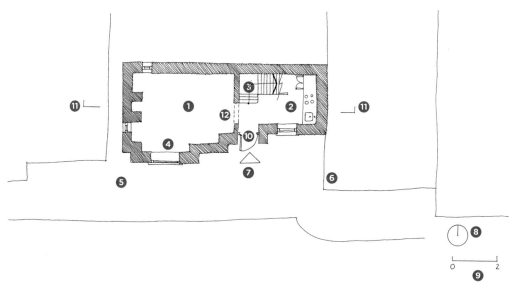

1. Label every room.

2. Add furniture and important fixtures (such as kitchen units).

3. Include an arrow to indicate the direction of a staircase: always going up.

4. Views out? Ventilation? Annotate functions of openings.

5. Select and draw materials for the exterior landscaping.

6. Include the neighbouring buildings – there can never be enough context.

7. Access. How will occupants get in, out of and around the building? Highlight the main entrance.

8. Add a north point and, where possible, orientate your plan so that north is pointing upwards (or, if in the southern hemisphere, south is upwards).

9. Insert a scale, such as 1:50 (or a scale bar if the drawing is to be issued electronically, as shown on the drawing opposite).

10. Ensure all doors and entrances are clearly shown and do not clash with other building functions.

11. Indicate where the sections (see p. 104) are cut.

12. Dashed lines indicate there is an element above, such as a mezzanine (a floor between two others) or a void in the ceiling.

THE NORTH POINT

This simple little addition to the plan is essential. Without it there is an increased likelihood of confusion and a fair chance that the building will be constructed facing the wrong direction. A little circle with a line scribing the radius to the topmost edge is all that is required. North points are required only on plans. (In the southern hemisphere a south point is used.)

THE SECTION

A section is possibly the most important architectural drawing. You should cut sections through places in the plan where there is vertical change – i.e. through staircases, voids and double-height spaces, as well as through other features inside a building such as courtyards. The section reveals the spatial qualities of the proposal and can also show the wall construction, if required. You should also cut a section where the building envelope changes shape or direction, so with complex forms a section may be required every metre (every 3 feet).

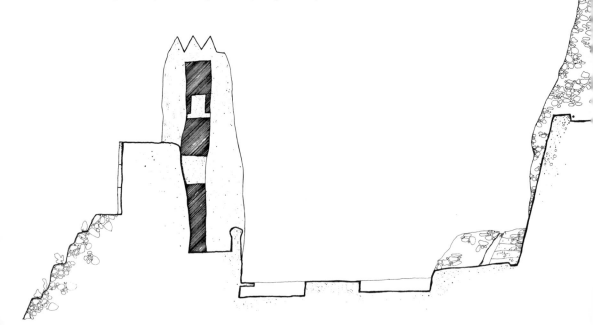

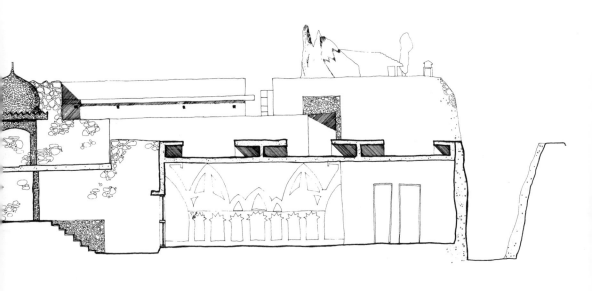

THE ELEVATION

The elevation shows how the building looks from the outside. Each side, or face, of the building is drawn separately, to scale, and without any perspective, as if the viewer is equidistant from all parts of it. Very few buildings are ever viewed purely in elevation, but it serves as a useful drawing for thinking about the appearance of the building.

Include materials and, most importantly, shading to denote shadows. A good elevation drawing, despite being a flat image, should convey the 3D aspects of a building. Without shadows the elevation will look very 'flat' and, more importantly, it will be difficult to discern from the drawing which components of the façade are in front of or behind others.

For example, on the image opposite, the windows appear set back from the main wall, because the eye interprets the thicker black lines as shadows, and the small triangular shadows cast by the dormer windows reveal that the main roof is pitched. I'm not suggesting that this building is a good piece of architecture, but it does reveal a couple of good principles to follow: the façade is arranged into seven vertical bays – an odd number of bays always looks better than an even one. The central bay is increased in height to denote the location of the entrance, but this bay would work equally well if placed off centre. Horizontally the building is split into top, middle and bottom sections. This is a good way to think about your elevational treatment and layout.

Should the façade express the internal functions or should it be designed independently of what takes place inside?

DRAW THE BUILDING IDEA IN 20 SECONDS

If you cannot explain and sketch your building design idea within 20 seconds then it is either too complex or you have not sufficiently resolved it.

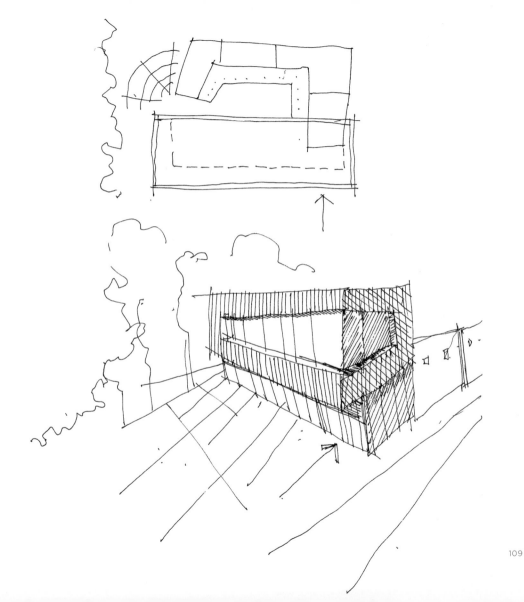

PEOPLE

Add people to your drawings, especially on elevations. They help to indicate scale, show how the space might be used and add some 'life' to the work. A well-populated drawing also gives the impression that the space will be successful, busy and lucrative – so always include crowds of people on drawings when presenting to clients and investors. Kite-flyers and dog walkers are a must.

THE GRID

The grid is a powerful design tool, conceptual aid and organizational device. Use a grid to help compose façades and the layouts of structural columns or walls. You should also employ it to inform your presentation layouts. A grid need not result in uniformity or banal repetition – it will bring cohesion and clarity to your work. At a city scale, grids are used to organize space and to define parcels of land. Le Corbusier's plan of Chandigarh in India, for example, exploits a grid to form the road networks, but within each sector there are smaller non-grid-based routes.

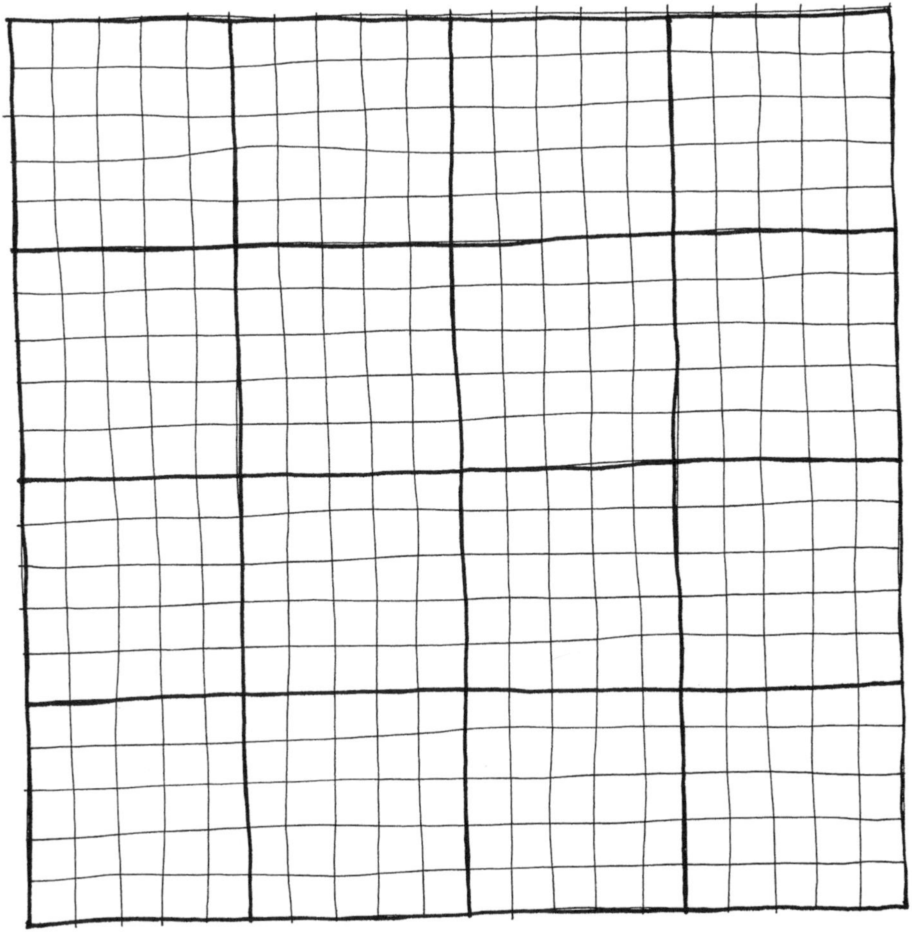

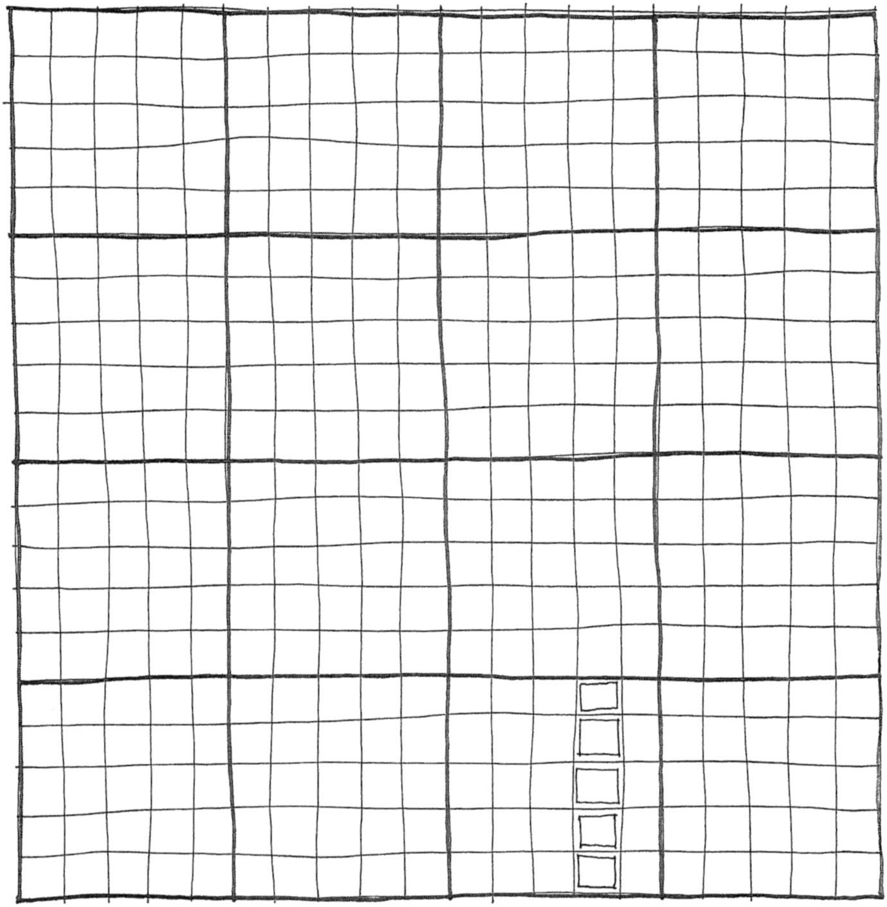

UPSETTING THE GRID

Once you have established a grid don't be afraid of introducing an element that upsets it or disrupts its uniformity. You can denote emphasis and playfulness through some simple additions or subtractions. For example, when using a grid to lay out a façade, you could highlight an entrance or staircase to break down the formality.

PROCESS

CONTEXT

Responding to context should not result in mediocrity and deference to what has been built previously. Remember that your design proposal is for a specific place and always include the wider context on your elevational drawings. Some students just include a couple of metres or feet of buildings, or space, on either side of their proposal, but try to stretch this to at least the city block or street. The more context you add to your drawings the better they will look.

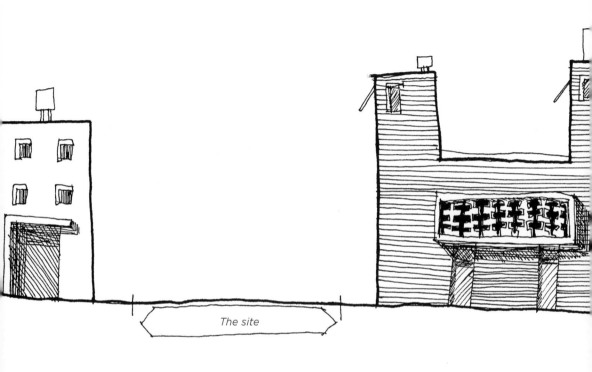

The site

GHASTLY GOOD TASTE

Why do you like the things, styles and appearances that you do? What has informed those decisions? Trust your ability to judge what is good and bad taste – but also hone your taste through a sound knowledge of history, technology and current trends. Be prepared to design what others think of as ghastly. Don't automatically reject the popular, pastiche or commonplace. Modernism and minimalism do not always equal good.

CEREMONY, MYTHS AND RITUALS

So much of architecture is connected to a notion of procession: most great buildings incorporate a sense of ritual or journey that the visitor experiences as he or she moves through a series of choreographed and curated spaces. Think about the spatial experience and the emotions you wish to stir in the visitor as he or she journeys through your design. We have become overly concerned with form. An exciting form is not as *architectural* as an exciting space that is experienced. The three journeys opposite all lead towards an artefact, but achieve the same result in three different ways.

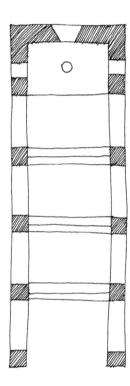

Colonnade, open procession

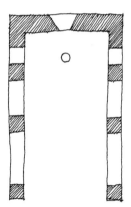

Short and rapid but also intimate

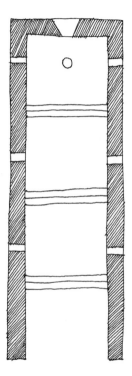

Enclosed, dark and mysterious

DON'T REDUCE ARCHITECTURE TO JUST SPACE, FORM AND LIGHT

Sometimes we compartmentalize architecture: we think of materials, structure and services as somehow distinct from it, rather than being fully integral to it. Equally, we should not think of things as 'mere' detail or town-planning – it is all architecture. Read the list below out loud – meditate on these truths.

ARCHITECTURE IS STRUCTURE
ARCHITECTURE IS MATERIALS
ARCHITECTURE IS DETAIL
ARCHITECTURE IS TOWN-PLANNING

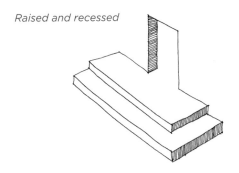

Raised and recessed

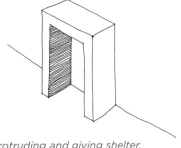

Protruding and giving shelter, delaying the entry moment

FRONT–BACK/ PUBLIC–PRIVATE

Try to distinguish between what is front and public, and what is back and private. This will help you to organize your plan and your elevational treatments. We should be able to recognize the front and the entrance of a building without signage.

Entrances should be integral to the façade design, but they are often enhanced if they are raised, protrude or are recessed.

FOCUS

Eye-catchers, landmarks and axes (imaginary, fixed straight lines) are useful in drawing attention from afar and serving as a beacon to draw people in or to distract their attention, or to provide visual delight. An axis is ceremonial and linear and, with a clear beginning, the destination always remains in view. The eye-catcher is less formal and is more about exploration and discovery. It plays 'hide and seek', offering glimpses to the viewer but then disappearing behind a wall or landscape – it can be thought of as an architectural burlesque.

❶ Start of the journey
❷ Break in wall gives view of the temple
❸ View from the temple to the boat sheds and lake
❹ Grottoes to be discovered

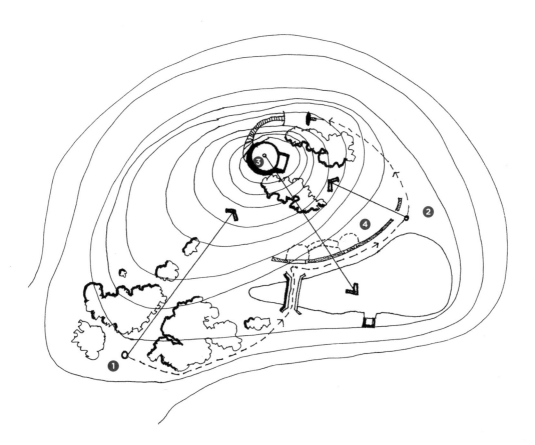

THE SPACES BETWEEN

The spaces created between forms need to be designed. Create spaces
for exchange, meeting and people-watching. These spaces need to
be protected from the wind, provided with rain/sun shelter and to be
overlooked so that they feel safe. They should be in places that people
want to move through, rather than tucked away and not part of a main
thoroughfare. Steps can also become seats, planters can double as
tables and subtle changes in materials can demarcate boundaries.
Design internal spaces for chance encounters – encourage gossip
spots and impromptu meeting-places.

THE CHRONOLOGICAL DRAWING

The purpose of a chronological drawing is to represent how a building, space, street or city has developed over time. You could, of course, use a map to show how buildings and streets have come and gone – but that cannot convey the same narratives as a chronological drawing. The drawing of Chandigarh below, by recording the gradual shift in styles, attempts to show the evolution (or narrative) of a district.

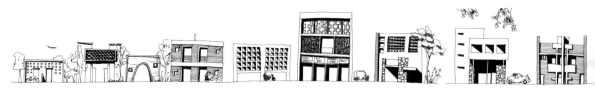

1950s

1960s

1980s

THE SERIAL VIEW

The serial view shows movement through a space. Think of each drawing as being a key frame in a film. The aim is to show the views we experience and encounter whilst we progress along a journey through a building. Three sketches are shown here, but a drawing for a serial view can be made every 5 metres (16 feet).

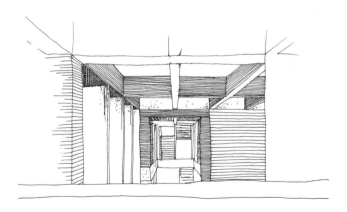

THE THRESHOLD

The threshold is the point at which one space ends and another one begins. Be aware of and attempt to set boundaries within your scheme. A doorway is the most obvious example of a threshold, but other, more permeable and less tangible thresholds can be created through changes in level, material and volume. Use the threshold to organize space and to create distinct zones of activity. How do we determine territories, boundaries and spatial ownership?

1 *A wall:* even though the space may not have a door or a roof, the presence of a wall implies ownership and privacy. This is perhaps the most blunt form of threshold.

2 *Materials:* by simply using a different flooring material a threshold can be created and boundaries, implying ownership and territory, defined.

3 *Markers:* these are simple objects placed to define an edge. A line of small stones is all that it takes to create an enclosure.

4 *Ponds/moats/ditches:* just as adding material to form a wall creates a threshold, so does its removal. Reflecting pools placed in front of a building are very effective – they make the building look taller and, in hot climates, can also help to keep it cool.

5 *Planting and vegetation:* the living fence can not only define space it can also be a defensive barrier.

6 *Changes in height:* the space on either side of the staircase seems to 'belong' to it.

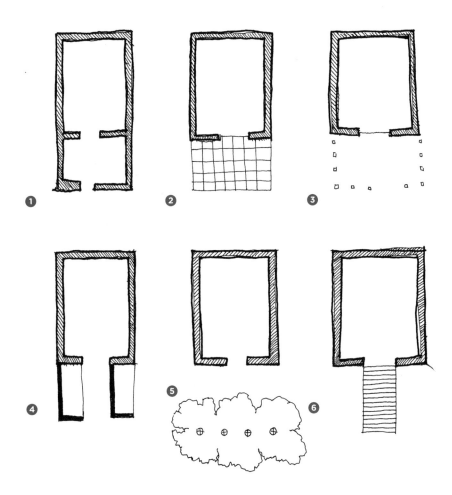

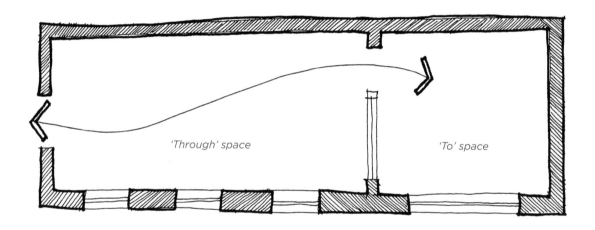

'Through' space

'To' space

'THROUGH' SPACES AND 'TO' SPACES

Certain spaces we pass through, others are destinations. 'To' spaces feel more secure and restful. They tend to have only one entrance and/or exit. A 'through' space is more dynamic, offers opportunity for exchange and encounter, and usually serves as a hub from which other activities stem. Living rooms and bedrooms tend to be 'to' spaces as they feel more secure. 'Through' spaces are more difficult to plan as a portion of the space is always lost to circulation.

THE PEDESTAL

The pedestal is a way of highlighting the significance and prestige of a particular object or element.

❶ At its most basic, the pedestal is used to celebrate an artefact and to make it easier to view. The size of the pedestal in relation to the object on display is important. Recess the base of the pedestal so that it appears to float (and will not get kicked and scuffed when people approach it).

❷ At a larger scale, buildings can also be set on pedestals. In a domestic house setting the ground floor is raised to create a grander entrance, a better view from inside and increased privacy.

❸ The 'tower and pedestal' model also works well, enabling a smaller, more human-scaled street front. Stepping back the tower allows more light to reach the street level and also helps visually to give the tower an appropriate base.

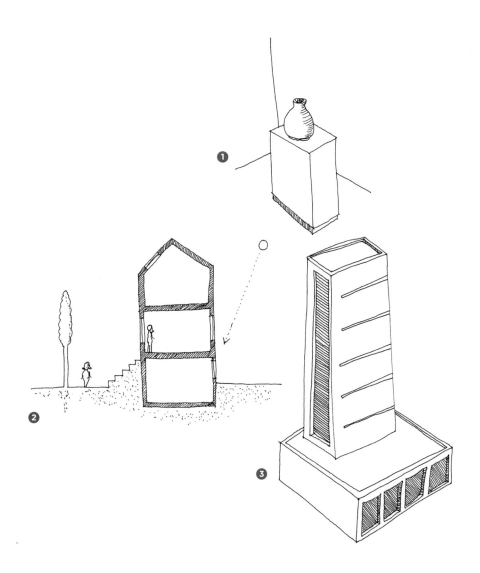

FORM, TECHNOLOGY AND PROGRAMME

A successful design needs to address form (the shape), programme (the functional demands) and technology (the problems of making). If one of these factors is neglected the entire concept is in danger of collapse. These three components also exist within a certain place, time and society, which also need to be carefully considered and acknowledged.

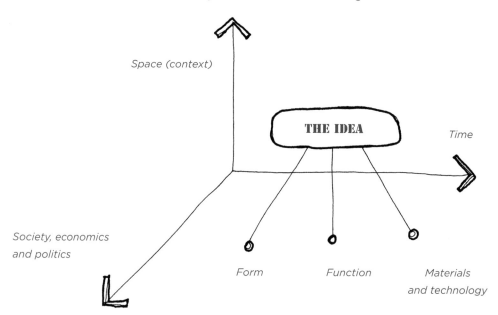

Space (context)

THE IDEA

Time

Society, economics and politics

Form

Function

Materials and technology

COST, TIME AND QUALITY

These are the three factors that control most architectural commissions. Your client can only have two out of the three:

If they want the project completed quickly and to a high quality it is going to cost a lot.

If they want a high-quality project for a good price it is going to take a long time to design and deliver.

If they want the project cheap and quick it is not going to be very good quality.

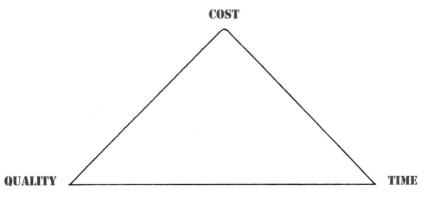

MAKING PROGRESS

VERBAL PRESENTATION

The critique is a daunting but very important aspect of becoming an architect. Plan your presentation and rehearse what you are going to say. Your presentation should tell a story with the most important drawings at the eye-level of the critics. Make sure that your drawings can be read from 2 metres (6 feet) away and are well-lit and carefully arranged – no curling edges or poorly laid out sheets. Ensure that your models are properly displayed and that you bring along all your sketchbooks.

Digital presentations need even more planning so that your explanation is coherent and you are not flipping back and forth through your slides. Clarity and simplicity are the key. Try to avoid reading your presentation and, instead, use your drawings as cues. Be brave and confident – look your critics in the eye and try to enjoy the moment. Get a friend to jot down the key discussion points so that you don't immediately forget them following the post-critique party.

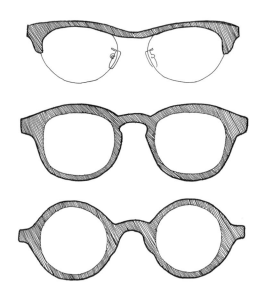

DRESS AND STYLE

A lot of architects wear only black clothes. Like other people who adopt this attire (magicians, undertakers, clergy) they are solemn, earnest and ritualistic. You can take a more expressive and flamboyant path. Think about how you look and dress. Develop (or reinvent) a style that becomes indistinguishable from who you are as a designer.

ARCHITECTURE IS ABOUT PEOPLE

Many talented designers forget this, or let arrogance get in the way. We should never forget that we are designing for and with people. Architects need to get on with a large team: engineers, contractors and developers, all of whom have conflicting desires and objectives. The structural engineer is generally concerned only with the structure, the electrician really cares only about the cable runs and the quantity surveyor views everything in terms of its cost – the only person to holistically consider the entire composition is the architect.

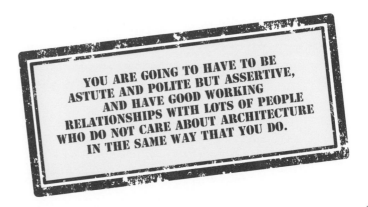

YOU ARE GOING TO HAVE TO BE ASTUTE AND POLITE BUT ASSERTIVE, AND HAVE GOOD WORKING RELATIONSHIPS WITH LOTS OF PEOPLE WHO DO NOT CARE ABOUT ARCHITECTURE IN THE SAME WAY THAT YOU DO.

BUT DON'T WORK FOR THE FOLLOWING PEOPLE ...

The best way to learn about architecture is to attempt to design a building. Opportunities will come, but the following client groups need to be treated with some caution.

Husband and wife clients – make sure you charge at least double fees. You will spend considerable time acting as a marriage counsellor and negotiating between both parties.

Gangsters/nightclub owners – hold back at least one key drawing until the final fee payment has been made.

Complex client structures – whether you are working for a school, corporation, or local authority, there is a tendency for the 'client body' to grow into a large and complicated committee structure. Always identify who the decision-maker is and only accept instructions from one person. It may take time for decisions to be agreed, so ensure that a clear timetable is formulated and that answers to your questions will be provided within a set period.

Developers wanting 'feasibility' drawings up to planning-approval stage – avoid working for free on the promise of further work to follow. If you give away your work for free it is effectively worthless, and why should you shoulder the risk of someone else's enterprise?

'Can you just ...' – these enquiries generally come from acquaintances who want you to *just* do some drawings for their house extension, or to offer advice on their dilapidated and buddleia-infested house. It is good to be friendly and helpful but do not devalue the profession and your education by working for nothing. Set proper fees, always have professional indemnity insurance and seek out wealthy clients who value architecture and the contribution you can make to their projects.

SCHEDULING YOUR WORKLOAD AND PLANNING FOR KEY MILESTONES AND LIFESTYLE BALANCE

One of the 'rites of passage' at architecture school is doing a so-called all-nighter. This means that you stay in the studio working on your project all night long, fuelled by energy drinks and caffeine tablets; sometimes several all-nighters are completed on consecutive nights. These times can be good fun but they are rarely productive. Instead, plan your workload, make every hour count, and set daily and weekly targets. Many students fill eight hours with a task that should have taken two hours. Spending every hour in the studio is unhealthy and not sustainable. It also makes you a dull and unhygienic studio-mate. Eat fresh food, shower frequently, go for a run, visit a gallery, have non-architect friends. Spending more than 12 hours per day in the studio is tedious and detracts from your development as a designer and thinker.

WHEN IS THE
NEXT CRITIQUE?
HOW MANY DAYS DO YOU HAVE
LEFT AND HOW MANY DRAWINGS
AND/OR MODELS NEED TO BE
COMPLETED PER DAY?

WHERE DO YOU STAND?

It is quite possible for you to disagree with and to make a counter-argument to every point made in this book.

QUESTION EVERYTHING
DON'T BLINDLY FOLLOW FASHIONS
OR DOGMATIC DISCOURSE.
ADOPT A POSITION AND KNOW
YOUR OWN MIND.

INDEX

ACKNOWLEDGEMENTS

Most of what is included in this brief booklet was passed on to me by the teachers, architects, technologists and clients that I've worked with.

In particular, I'm grateful to Souymen Bandyopadhyay, Stephen Bell, Jack Dunne, James Burke, David Dunster, Mike Knight, Barry Lewis, Bill Lowe, Emma Mitchell, Ian Nahapiet, Robert Plant, David Roocroft, Anja Schade, Torsten Schneiderknecht, Ola Uduku and Anas Younes.

YOU CANNOT DO ARCHITECTURE ON YOUR OWN LEARN TO WORK WITH OTHERS AND ALWAYS ACKNOWLEDGE THE HELP THAT YOU RECEIVE ALONG THE WAY. THERE ARE VERY FEW NEW IDEAS – THE REST ARE JUST VARIATIONS ON THEMES AND MINOR INCREMENTAL DEVELOPMENTS.